Contains
Mild Peril

In memory of
Frederick Paul Buckner
1928–2006

Contains Mild Peril

Adrian Buckner

Five Leaves Publications
www.fiveleaves.co.uk

Contains Mild Peril

Adrian Buckner

Published in 2008 by Five Leaves,
PO Box 8786, Nottingham NG1 9AW
info@fiveleaves.co.uk
www.fiveleaves.co.uk

Five Leaves acknowledges financial support from
Arts Council England

Cover illustration:
The Orchard by Paul Nash
©Tate, London 2007

Design and typesetting by
Four Sheets Design and Print Ltd.

Printed in Great Britain

ISBN: 978 1 905512 43 0

Five Leaves is a member of Inpress (www.inpressbooks.co.uk),
representing independent publishers.

Contents

Poems

Literary
Society

The Folded Poems

Your poems have been folded several times.
You smoke when typing them,
probably when packing them up
into this envelope
which flopped onto my mat this morning.
I think my mat is not the first.

You are wary of the new neighbours.

You feel helpless in the face of illness.

Why do you admire anglers who say nothing?

Neither can I hazard as to how
the young will learn manners.

There is a crumbling mountain of Tippex
on the sonnet's fourth line
into which *steely eyed*
is carved in blotchy blue
in front of *yearning.*

You have always blamed governments.

You are beginning to blame women.

Dickens in the Afternoon

to the memory of non-vocational Adult Education

There is a piano in the corner. Perhaps
the stool is to be found in the cupboard;

the cupboard where, the note attached
to the key informs me,

some folding tables may be found
should there not be enough in Room 3.

I am advised against opening the windows;
should I encounter any difficulties

I am to call Jean who will try to contact Arthur
who will be coming later to lock up.

I rub a Georgian shop window
from the blackboard, detach

from the flipchart a sheet inscribed:
Computers for the Terrified, Monday 11am.

No thank you. Modern life makes
us nervous enough. We prefer

Oliver Twist on Tuesday afternoons.
And when we have settled on which page

Chapter 38 begins in our various editions,
we can address today's proposition:

Dickens hoped and believed the instincts
of the well born and the public spirited

would bring England the good society.
I think we will hope it too.

Deliver us into Textbooks

I can promise a deepening sense of the reasonableness of the human past and thus a modest confidence in the future.

DENYS HAY — PREFACE TO 'THE MEDIEVAL CENTURIES' (1952)

We have no truck
with your twentieth century analysis,

admiring as we do individuals of substance: an Emperor,
barefoot in the snow, penitent before a Pope.

Localised agonies stretching
for half a century can disappear into the spine

as long as each chapter concludes with a flowering
of culture, a first breath of enlightenment

or the once and for all vanquishing of an enemy
be it religious, dynastic or continental.

Take this consolation from us: for four centuries
life was grim. Then things began to pick up —

a world fit for textbooks to be written,
that has been our end.

11

Early English

Two thickened-out matchstick figures
about to enter the Abbey: Father and Son,
Teacher and Pupil on page fifty one
of *The Observer's Book of Architecture.*

"Son, tiny though you are, I will lead you
with my left hand and with my right raised,
indicate to you this beautiful example
of The Early English flying buttress.

For there are certain sensibilities, fields
of knowledge which I, as your Father
have a duty to cultivate in you. An instinctive
grasp of them will keep you from going to the bad."

My too-modern mind nailed the sub-text
then eagerly fell on the *explanatory* text.
It's all a question of your perspective,
but mostly a simple one of scale.

The Orwell Readers

Three months after you died I read
The Road to Wigan Pier.

If either of us happened to be reading Orwell
it would be part of our weekly phone call.

We didn't say or think anything startling,
admiring him in the way he is generally admired:

the beauty of the plain style, the prescience,
the clear eye on the English character.

Your dying is complicated. I do not want
to divide it up into twenty

simple questions hoping to go unanswered
so they can turn themselves into poems.

Some things were said, others weren't;
some things resolved, others not.

Nothing more common. A dozen families
in this town could be leaving it there

this very morning. But I woke, thinking
how we both loved Orwell and knew why.

Perhaps he could have looked at us
and written down in two pages

what we were, you to me and me to you,
and how we fitted in.

Literary Society

Everybody in this room loves everybody
else in this room, passing together

our late, late middle age. Our eyes
grow milder, our bellies softer

and some of us doze through more
than the AGM. No offence

is taken among friends who shall all
have their time to doze — dreaming

of other rooms, book-lined, smoky
where our youthful wordy swagger

won the cutest of points from
our sage and elder betters; of days

when we fell out over books, made up,
but never because it was *just* a book;

of days when we knew
that lit.crit. was life itself.

Difficult to say if we're disappointed.
Desmond rages from time to time,

but affable appearances are mostly kept up.
After all, we have a policy: Visitors are Welcome.

And we were once visited by a young man
from the Council's Arts Department,

but if truth be told, we never got to grips
with "Audience Development", our talents

lying as they do in another direction —
the development and delivery

of the wittiest, most courteous, most urbane
and most elegantly articulated

Vote of Thanks.

The Course Not Viable

WEA Evening Class, Nottingham 2005

I'm informed at Reception that a third gentleman
has enquired. I will wait for another eight
to take this road through February sleet.

David is the second of two:
"I could be seven people, I like
seven types of poetry. Does that help?"

"Lovely idea" says our Branch official —
specs, corduroys and shyly brightening
with the slow smile of a lifetime's gentle behaviour.

No calling for execution, his instinct's
to console. He stays to make a four
for what the office calls 'a taster'.

I joke feebly about sixty years' poetry in an hour,
decide against Douglas's *How To Kill*
and give out James Wright's *The Blessing* instead.

— Later on the bus, I remember
I had Larkin in reserve.
Who will be the last, the very last? —

Gradually we find ways of talking
about things other than poetry. At the close
we shake hands in the foyer,

David says in morale-boosting style
that he specialises in finding oases
and then moving on to the next desert.

When the moment presents, I do not suggest
the pub or point in the listings to dates
for open mic poetry and creative writing courses —

15

we did not come to pluck from that sexy
fruiting tree "The City's Cultural Offer";
we did not come to be vibrant, seek new opportunities;

we came to do this once a week,
saw there were not enough of us, spoke a blessing,
brushed up on wistful irony and left.

At the Small Press Festival

Two young women told me they had ME.
A sixty year old Poet declared himself out of fashion.

Another bragged cheerfully: "I confine myself
these days to brief and bitter squibs of envy."

A Theatre Director of frightening energy
bought four back copies, mislaid them, returned

to buy again in a fluster of apology and goodwill
that left me squishy for all of womankind

(a morale booster cancelled out by the man making
a particular effort to return one of my free leaflets).

An hour later, contemplating my £2.75, I was roused
by a return visit from one of the afflicted females

who promised to try to send me some poems.
I dallied briefly with the idea that Virginia Woolf

had made an improper suggestion, then woke
to a survey of my optimistic stack.

I decided the coffee smelt good. On the positive,
I nearly covered my petrol and am growing to understand

a series of interrupted conversations with semi-interested parties
as (in a very real sense) *invaluable networking.*

17

Early Hughes

At fifteen we hadn't cared
for Shakespeare read out loud,
by rote "renderings" of Chaucer
or leanings on a coppice gate;

fanning from *Lycidas*,
dense with ancient pencil
to thirty pages of notes.
And then came early Hughes,

prowling around our nerve ends
and built to last
like a briefcase kicked about the yard.
Tyrone said Mr L, *What is the poet saying?*

Sir, the poet's saying this pig is dead.
Anything else? He's saying Sir, this pig
is really, like completely
fucking dead.

Thank You Something Paul Muldoon

(after reading "Winter Wheat")

I couldn't meet the workshop
deadline, spent Saturday pestering
one image about patches
of grass scuffed
in the dog days of August.

As for the rest — well,
there were a lot of somethings.
Something about a stick
being lobbed into a tree;
something about a fast-living urban raspberry,

a blowsy, exhausted, no-better-than-she-should-be dahlia
and of course plenty of something somethings
that touched on sex, aesthetics and decadence.
At one point, the senses got mixed up —
that really was something.

I briefly toyed with something
of a reprise, kept returning to the grass.
I should have left the grass at home.
A polite *Oh, how interesting*
would have tidied it away for good —

a little insignificant something
of my own, contentedly unattached
to a more important something.
So Thank You Paul Muldoon for something
Very Like An Inferiority Something.

Reading on a Train:
Poetry in the Making by Ted Hughes

How beautiful it is,
that eye-on-the-object look.   W.H. AUDEN

The winter sun, unbroken
through four hours
of my journey south.
We are quiet and we are few
on the Sunday cross country train.

> *He stands at the opening*
> *of each chapter, a teacher*
> *before his chosen audience*
> *of undistracted children*
> *who have yet to write a line.*

> *Peer for the clutter-piercing detail*
> *that brings this thing alive;*
> *write about an animal,*
> *a person you know*
> *and a person you don't.*

A fragile weave,
this afternoon's content.
Three parts of luck in place:
this book, this sun,
the comfort of this train.

> *The simple,*
> *ravishing question:*
> *What are they doing,*
> *those people,*
> *staring at the sea?*

> *Words are not the same*
> *as the things*
> *that happen to you.*
> *Bridge the gap,*
> *"we call it poetry."*

At Poole a seventy year old man
crouches to embrace and point
his granddaughter across the harbour.
Both their scarves blow
in both their faces.

    I feel my luck holding,
    my clutter four hours north.

The 1st XI

A Village Cricketer Considers Himself

Here I stand, midwicket saving one,
though I am rather more attached

to my grander and recently
re-acquired status of cultural icon —

it keeps my mind off that nostril-pierced
daughter of mine and her friends;

helps me forget the mortgage, the meeting
on Monday, that bloody gearbox.

All things considered I would rather
be viewed as a white eternal spirit

forever walking in with the bowlers of England
across one boundless village green

than be seen and heard
living this life I live.

And if all this sounds as outlandish
as a Prime Minister's re-election stunt

let me at least be seen today
from a passing express train

about to execute the perfect cover drive,
orientating myself composedly

under the highest skyer, becoming
a split second enigma for those

who, slumped and gazing through glass,
discover that England has occurred to them.

After John Major (1992), George Orwell (1941)

25

Cricket at Thrumpton

Lined up behind boundary flags
a fleet of Renault, Nissan and Ford;
only one or two from the village now
close enough to pedal or walk.

One of the old hands regrets the lack
nowadays of spectating wives and kids —
"Folk just don't have the time — always
something else they'll need or find to do."

The midday heat unfurls across a balmy
late afternoon — what fades for an hour or two
is the significance of change — absorbed
like tomorrow's heat into a reddening sky.

Long past the casting of the die, the game
ambles on without a trace of impatience;
courtesies are exchanged between men of sixteen
and sixty, a little light applause

for a manful effort at an impossible catch.
Something, eroding perhaps, is being passed on
as an unseen cow lumbers over to chew
the wing mirror of the fast bowler's Mondeo.

Calling the Game Off

Six of us in the middle of life,
in the middle of the field,

ruminating on a deferred
abandonment of hope,

grazing on a
diminishing chance.

Machines that spike and absorb
have been hauled out to join us

but lie idle, somehow
not quite to the point

when we have arms to fold,
thumbs to press turf,

eyes to raise, shoulders
to look over.

Pessimism is plain food,
relished in silence, nourishing

like a confident prediction
of a cloud bank's course.

Gestures wither to a damp
shuffling. Agreement is unspoken.

A sudden shower
is an unnecessary drama

bringing to an end
the argument we were not having.

We like this more than we let on,
could have sustained another hour

together, but move apart now
into our differing landscapes.

Love of Cricket

was born in me through prolonged
consideration of the weather;
such sweet requital if the rain should stop.

The eight stone Indian, three-sweatered
at Hove in April. Magic in those spinning fingers
if June could warm them.

The Barbadian, wrists of steel
and the touch of silk. I watched him kick his heel
and look at the grey Worcestershire sky.

The Australian, man mountain at ease
under the baggy green cap. Huge with threat,
he didn't care about the weather.

"The Pathan Warrior", idly
foot fussing the damp sawdust;
a whole summer to break sweat and stumps.

When the sun came through it would be pale.
Down the steps would come a young man —
tall, handsome, gifted, but nonetheless

a little like me. And defying stoutly
the wily, brawny charisma of the world
he'd ensure England would never, ever, lose.

For CMJ

It started for me in '71: rumours
of an Indian with a withered arm
running through England at the Oval —
"Chandra", the conjuring, chantable
abstract of Bhagwat Chandrasekhar.

The following June,
my ear to a radio with batteries wearing down —
Boycott taking Lillee's first over after rain delay.
I ran back to school, wondering
about bad light, an early lunch, a seamer's paradise.

From that moment, it was all epic to me.
You confirmed it on the page:

England Expects you wrote
when Boycott stepped out again
to open at Port of Spain

and when he mis-hooked Boyce
with only six on the board
the ball hung in the air for half a page.

Grincote Cricket Club 1949–2005

Chairman	*J.D. Laird*
Secretary	*J.D. Laird*
Fixture Secretary	*J.D. Laird*
Welfare Officer	*J.D. Laird*
I do not know you	J.D. Laird
but I'm guessing	J.D. Laird
Groundsman	J.D. Laird
Wicket Preparation	J.D. Laird
Subscription Collector	J.D. Laird
Fundraiser	J.D. Laird
Prize Donator	J.D. Laird
Ground Opener	J.D. Laird
Ground Closer	J.D. Laird
Score Box Maker	J.D. Laird
Stump Mender	J.D. Laird
Line Painter	J.D. Laird
Lift Giver	J.D. Laird
Drinks Buyer	J.D. Laird
Drinks Maker	J.D. Laird
Sandwich Cutter	J.D. Laird
Kit Handler	J.D. Laird
Scorecard Checker	J.D. Laird
Parent Pacifier	J.D. Laird
Agenda Setter	J.D. Laird
Minute Taker	J.D. Laird
Nurofen Carrier	J.D. Laird
Head Scratcher	J.D. Laird
Head Against Wall	J.D. Laird
Emergency Meeting Convenor	J.D. Laird
Hospital Check-Up	J.D. Laird
Does No One Else Care	J.D. Laird?

I do not know you
did you labour
with saintly non complaint?
or did you
drive the others away?

For your mark at the crease
Here's to you
For your last wicket stand
God save you

J.D. Laird

J.D. Laird

J.D. Laird

J.D. Laird

Autopoet

Summer again —

slicks of dog piss
link up the wheelie bins;

sash windows roll out
the bitter domestic.

Conspiring with the blare
of the season's hit record,

the sound of poverty
scrapping in its backyard.

You yearn for rain
to sweep humankind
and its litter away —
but waiting,

lyricise it all
because three Asian boys
play cricket
on the crossroads

until mother umpire
in gold and maroon
shepherds them in
for the light.

After Rain

Sodden and pale
the lawn where the children played

save the bare darkened patch
where the young hero's bat

tapped the turf into dust
from lunchtime to dusk.

I taste in my tea
the just turned milk,

stare and savour
the wound in the turf —

how it will mend,
is mending already.

I pad around outside,
tip a chair to hear

pooled water sliding
onto the paving stones.

My son appears, warm
and thick with sleep;

for five minutes he squats
to coax a snail.

I pick two cherries,
beaded with rain —

one just ripe,
the other dark and splitting,

its wound
dry as yesterday.

Wound

A man and a child, one bat and a ball,
an hour a day on a council-cut verge.

By August's end two bare patches marked
the batter's crease and the bowler's line.

The boy went back to school, father worked
till Christmas Eve, but looked each morning

for the blemish on the grass, in his mind
a sweet incommunicable wound,

persisting under his watch past the fall,
awaiting the covering balm of snow.

Cultural Exchange

Twenty years in Dad's loft,
the last box of those books
I hoovered up from eleven to fifteen:

My Life in Cricket;
Bowling for Boys;
The Fight for the Ashes 1972.

Men with solid averages and good wars,
prescribing remedial action
to arrest "the decline of our beautiful game".

The Rt. Reverend Warner
demonstrates his back defence
to the short pitched ball

and the Nawab remembers
meeting Monty
and opening for Harrow at Lords.

                                ***

I kept four —
for stylistic reasons now —
offered the rest to *Wren's Antiquarian Books and Prints.*

Fifteen quid the lot.
I picked up the cash
on the way to the Multiplex with the kids:

Three for *Jungle Book 2*
and a regular carton of Fanta.
£13.60. Keep the change.

Suburban Memory

It was the kind of afternoon
when the garden needs the rain;

when you look at the lawn's deep green
and the red brick of next door's back;

learn from a TV documentary
how a cricket ball is stitched.

The kind of afternoon when only
The old are at home and stay indoors,

watch folk through the net curtains,
make tea for one and water the plants.

It was the kind of day
that slows down after half past one

with reposeful thoughts
of a husband passed on, a son up north;

the kind of afternoon I only took one sweet
and never forgot to say thank you

for the home-made jam and gardening hint
I'd always take home to mother.

On the Playground

The Innocents

Father MacNiece. Our American Priest.
On Sundays he came down from the pulpit,

opened the gate on the communion rail,
ambled his sermon up and down the aisle.

On Mondays he came into our classroom,
gave us little homilies on being good,

some great gags on falling a little short.
Slow smile, easy teasing.

One morning he ruffled my hair, saying
ain't that the truth, tiger?

And I've never found the words that pin
the warm shiver of joy, the blush inside

that I wanted to hug to myself as it pulsed
for a second more than I dared to hope.

Easter Falling

Good Friday morning. Careless of one difference
in this day — an altered bus schedule —

I'm under my umbrella, a one man queue
watching the rain that has come down for a week

come down again, my gaze narrowing
to the kerb's pulpy slick of litter.

No one passes nor walks on the other side;
all holds for two stilling, sufficient minutes

as I engage wholly, essentially, this passive waiting.
On the bus I do not read, nor ponder the tedium

of work that will not, can not stop,
but follow trails of beading rain, remembering

the child who mumbled the words all year
but at this time was stirred to sing.

Gone Away

Gone away, you say, then a worldly shrug
of two year old shoulders. Gone away,

the pigeons you chase in the park, the bee
that hovers fleetingly over

the unopened chalice of honeysuckle;
the fair leaving town this weekend.

You make no distinctions: *gone away*
takes them all, a vast encompassing destination

like the one road wide and endless
in a flat land. You stand at one end,

all around you what your eyes know
as the land of *come back.*

On the Playground

A mood reviews the options,
its parts manoeuvre for me

then call a truce — ease
and boredom merge, absorb

a small depression of spirit
presented by

the desultory litter
left by local truants.

I turn my eyes from a crushed can
to the top of the slide.

The here and now —
the willed passing of an afternoon,

or another mooring
in a tranquil harbour

that in a year
will be the heart of longing.

I close my eyes, feel the heat
on my upturned face —

*OK, you go and hide,
I'll count to ten.*

A Very Practical Criticism

Not exactly rigorous scrutiny
followed by dismissal from the canon,

more a pitiless peremptory
hurling onto the scrapheap.

My little ten month Leavisite, not walking
but cruising from chair to sofa

to second bookshelf height. Here they come,
pulled out, dropped or round arm flung:

Collected Shorter Auden — too thick, too white;
Naipaul's *India* — ditto and not deep enough blue;

The Brothers Karamazov — too heavy;
Poetry Review — can't get the leverage.

Ah! A row of slim Fabers, bookended by *Selected Lawrence* —
at last something to get one's two teeth into.

Early Critical Works

An all day rain day reaches four o'clock.
I gaze out to the lawn. My three year old

is occupied daubing fiery vermillion
on a steady supply of my old poems

in which love fails, graffiti disfigures
the playground, the powerless

voice their dramatic monologues
and feel no better for it.

He starts on the backs but soon dismisses
any distinctions my vanity might propose.

Drizzle anoints the creosoted fence —
I bore myself thinking it needs another coat.

He's moved onto crocus yellow,
but amid my foggy colours

even the lawn's lustre is a grey shade
around which words begin to cluster.

Nothing flowers

on the rented
squatted street
save repeating blooms
of tolerated smiles
into passing prams

and the hopeless
saving grace
of a child's scarf
pricked on a railing
at the padlocked nursing home

Lunch Party

Alcohol and sunshine had done their work,
the compact now in place —
adults and children could ignore each other
until dusk.

You filled our glasses, assumed melancholy
to regret one who couldn't be there,
thumbnailed his decline and concluded:
Character is Fate.

A hundred yards away your son
was enjoying a noisy triumph over one
who moved a little further off, fixing the heat behind his eyes
into the ground.

All Little Distances

You have been a year at school now
— all little distances
maturing into their enchantment:

mid afternoons
and a train heard a mile off;
then another two
before the need
to call you off the swing,
interrupt my noticings
of changes in the trees
and be somewhere else.

Browsing in the supermarket
as you slept,
the chance to learn names
for five varieties of pear.

Conkers were as cool as your cheeks
and leaves were kicked.

Best to avoid it,
the one hundred sonnet sequence
from *The Scan* through *First Steps*
and the grievous *Finding your Peg* —

just a few lines to keep for me
that precious interregnum of dawdling.

Yellow Hoop

For three years a yellow hoop has hung
in the schoolyard sycamore,

failing to nudge itself
up the caretaker's list of chores.

In the nude December tree
it is a hollowed sun

or if the mood takes,
a loose-limbed hurl from summer,

an exuberant infringement
of playground discipline.

Now in October, I watch for the yellow
to come through the changing yellow.

I point this out to my son — the age now
to remember things a year back.

In July I can say:
Do you remember what is behind the green leaves?

From school gate to classroom
it dignifies our progress

like a peculiar feature looked for
in the roof of the nave.

It will be a small violence
if one day the caretaker,

like the laziest of Cromwell's Visitors,
should decide to do his job.

Poems

Slabs and Ruins

That slab of walnut cake has beached me.
Here my journey ends, shuffling
round the National Trust Gift Shop, murmuring
outrage at the price of Country House Fudge.

A box of shortbread for the neighbours
who are looking after the cat, a souvenir pencil
for the children who irked me all afternoon
throwing a tennis ball at the Gothic ruin.

Twenty minutes ago I knew the difference between
a Decorated and a Perpendicular Spire;
twenty years ago I drank coffee from a flask
and sandwiches out of foil.

I have looked up three recommended food pubs,
conveniently located on the route back
to our hired Country Cottage with
easy access to the beautiful limestone landscape.

Last night I lay listening to the play of the beck,
a sting in its nimble delighting surge.
When did I join them? — the politely interested,
the leaflet fanciers, the slowly souring.

Desire assailed me: I would get up, follow the stream
into the valley. It failed in its moment
and I turned instead to Friday's plan,
weighing the merits of each available Castle.

Slow Burn

Left out and yellowing by the lounger,
Culture from the weekend broadsheet:

the bearded middle-aged columnist,
all chest, pocketed hands and brogues

stares out from his by-line,
finding more and more of life

less and less to his liking;
his words and gaze folded outwards

to slow burn, discolouring
with fertile spores of misanthropy.

At sundown the process is arrested —
words flap in the breeze

like the wasp, frantic for sweetness
at the bottom of the glass.

The Ancient Sunbather

He's not impressed by warnings
of a hole in the sky:

six weeks and not a drop of rain;
he is back in a golden age

of summers possessed undimmed
in his ageing heart.

He lies in the parched land
like a die hard colonist

sticking it out in Delhi after '47,
making a go of the new Rhodesia —

unmoved by forebodings of a world
falling in, a setting sun.

Easy Listening

The house empties, I retreat upstairs
to rest my eyes on the ceiling.

I have left music playing downstairs —
an annoyance surrendered

in the next moment's knowledge
that this is a perfect pitch:

low volume and poor tone, but reaching me
as consciousness slides, *Libera me*

and the successive grey horizons —
net curtain, sash window, slate roof and rain.

Brief Sleep

Ten to three. I was gone twenty minutes.
The carnations in the white vase
fill the next five, starlings
on pylons serve for two more.

On the second shelf down there's a blue
clothbound memoir. It changed my life
or how I thought about something
until my life changed again.

The rain outside is known as suburban
when watched through glass
on weekday afternoons: the little falling
into a life or making a garden grow —

never on a gale to blow fences down,
it feels like something settled for,
disclosing itself without comment
one afternoon in the middle of my life.

Summer Break

The heat was off me and had fallen
out of June. I dozed on the sofa,

under my eyelids a faint pulse
of first day Wimbledon drizzle.

Martina Hingis, veteran of twenty-six,
taking the opening set on the lushest green.

Virginia, can this artiste of the women's game
win Wimbledon again?

Let the question hang,
let a few more worries melt;

after today it's dust bowl on the baseline,
the clenched fist of victory,

something not thought of now
bawling out its deadline.

Lest We Channel Hop

Through the early months of Twenty 05
The Great War dragged on,
slugging through the schedule
between Lunchtime News and Tots TV.
Stalled, it dug in for weeks, stalemated
at World Snooker fortnight, Championship
Golf and Election Campaign Specials,
before heaving itself into May's final push.
Would it ever end? Life on the home front
was as normal, though sometimes,
they could be heard, above the boom
of suburban mowers, those daytime TV voices:
Redgrave narrating, Williams
as Lloyd George and Richardson, Haig.

On Expenses

This morning in *The Happy Eater,* a song
came on that I used to like; lulled

I gazed into space, let my coffee
go as cold as I sometimes let it go

looking at TV in my flat, slumped
shattered after a day on the road.

My heart wasn't in it today, I know
I've been ripped off over that shack in Hereford.

The M42 was murder, considered coming off
for a spin in the Cotswolds, but didn't —

time is short enough. Tonight I tried to write
to my son whom I'm no longer inclined to disown

but I couldn't find the words, so instead
I'm filling in my expenses claim, thinking

of him, halfway up a mountain, lost to me
as words are lost to me, as mountain air.

Dabbling In That Kind of Thing

I could fill a book with poems
from these things that come to mind.

You out of hospital again,
us, withdrawing for a few hours
to build sandcastles.

Defences weakening. Tides.

Our telephone conversation the next day:
you telling me you've planted out
those bulbs we brought down.

Grace note cosying up to melancholy.

Yes, I could fill a book
dabbling in that kind of thing.

Picking Up a Few Bits

Leaving the hospital we had fifty minutes to kill.
You took me down Dorchester's Roman Road
to *pick up a few bits* from the supermarket.
We were thinking the same
only differing in scale:
I did not think he would survive the weekend;
you, absorbing what you've seen,
were giving up on the prospect of one more year.

Before we reached the store
I looked to my left at a game of football,
canary yellow and blood red;
no fine display but a yeomanly struggle in the dusk
against the mud, the years.
And coming out with time still to spare
we paused to watch (I thought with a throb of warmth
how difficult it is *not* to stop for this).

Yellow's number 10 placed the ball on the penalty spot,
shot to the right and beat the dive of the goalie in grey.
Joyful, bedraggled, he peeled away towards us —
Oh Well Done!! you cried out,
hands clapping and on the balls of your feet,
the piercing whistle in the half dark,
the sparse, unfettered celebration on the touchline,
flooding my heart.

Poem

Sentence passed
on the last day of November:
with palliative care, two months.

She didn't deny them
their Christmas lights, but for herself,
nine lily stems, paring

a fortnight in their opening,
dropping pollen
on the white sills

which she left to stain
whilst looking at pictures
of the spring.

The Season of Daffodils

Three days after knowing the worst
she noticed the first bloom in her garden,

knew then that the season of his dying
would be the season of daffodils.

Each day showed her new abundance
in the town and hospital grounds

but she picked out the single flowers
cut down by winds insane with malice.

He was foul-mouthed, unbroken; the doctors
rational and kind; she'd hear them both out

then gaze outside to the teeming yellow —
all gains were relentless.

When the clusters began to ail
her eyes sought again the individual flowers

ravaged and tossed in a frenzy
of concentration to stay alive.

Jo

i.m Josephine Hannah Fagan

You are holding a potted geranium;
behind you, your tended forest.

Seventeen years after the fall
that snapped your six stone frame

your younger daughter passed to her sister
this forgotten black and white.

Within weeks the family windowsills
in the south and middle of England,

in County Cork and California,
hosted a new adornment.

Your children knew in an instant
that this was the one, not so much

for what it captured in you,
but that it captured for them

in your mild, peaceable indulgence
of the photographer's whim, that element

of repose they wished had embraced you
more often and for a little longer.

Passchendaele

I heard it right
but saw the letters wrong,

grew up believing
it was a given name —

that in a Flanders valley
the *everything men gave*

was a willing hurl
of desire, love and hope.

At fourteen, a little Owen
left my mistake intact.

Even now, watching the poppies
float from the roof of The Festival Hall

I follow the error through,
see it wrong again: Resurrection.

Antiquarian

I shove the door,
bring down the clatter of bells.
The bookseller sips coffee,
gazing on the road
looping its wet circular noise;
peace, chanced upon like clover
between leaves of *Dombey and Son;*
touch, satisfied
by the stiff discoloured flyleaf;
taste, the scent
of rain on my coat.

City Poet

In truth, I would have let it pass
had more effort been required
than a lunchtime stroll from the office
in late February sunshine.

One room in a museum, given over
for a month to commemorate him,
to dignify with municipal sentiment
our city's versifying hobo.

Words, pictures, a few possessions arranged
so we infer he had no desire for more.
Modest, he rated his achievement;
everything shown affirms that judgement.

The poems brief, a made point,
chained to a passing thought one day;
line drawings of familiar cityscapes,
sketches of those not working but roaming;

no piece more than twenty minutes'
musing from a marketplace seat,
all adding up to a protesting doodle
in the margin of the city's vivid page.

Difficult to know what else he did
apart from have thoughts he didn't put down,
get enough on dole to eat badly, drink well
and hold forth bardically at night.

But standing there in collar and tie,
compiling my cool assessment, I began
to feel stirred by what my eyes took in:
the voice, relentlessly minor, defeated

not in life but by this late acclaim
— *City Character, Bard of the street* —
which serves only to obscure something,
lowly perhaps, but at least his own stab at substance:

despair next to urgent hope, anger adjacent
to devils' laughter, stretched across so many
small canvases to a thin whimsy of pain
amid the city's indifferent midweek hum.

Reg

I hadn't seen you for nearly a year
then heard from your son

how one evening, walking down Sadler Gate
you'd been assaulted by two youths —

a fly kick to the back of the neck.
You were a bit shaken he said, not really hurt,

then added with that salty merriment
you've passed on:

my mother said she couldn't understand
why no-one had had the idea before.

When we met you waved away my concern,
preferring to grumble about war in Iraq,

and the Local History you're illustrating,
currently held up by another's dither.

I drank three pints, you sipped halves. Parting,
I watched you, past the statue of Bass,

up the steps of Derby Library,
under your arm an insect encyclopaedia

for your consultation with the entomologist
on the beetle you'd found in your flat.

The Girls on the Bus

come in pastels and white
from the morning's liquid sun

into a filled fetid space
stale with afternoon heat.

Beauty is outraged to witness
the unlinking of her maids,

sundered from each other's loveliness
for a dismal dusty minute.

Their eyes grieve for the loss, mourn
the offence, then flash in urgent alliance —

spines arch for the hunt:
a nod, one touch to the shoulder

and a synchronised fluttering dash
re-unite them on a vacant pair of seats.

Their smiles tip into laughter, joined
by the gods who see the world mended.

Work for Art's Sake

(after Bob Dylan's "Oh Sister")

The band pasted on the telephone booth,
the poem lost in a small magazine;
the painter exhibiting to the street
from his bay, the play upstairs in the pub;
the hand-written novel in the bottom drawer,
the framed print from the promising début.

I watch the city's lunchtime thousand
crossing the square from office and shop.

How many clutch such a secret to themselves?
and will they spill, to the busker in the subway
with a passion for Dylan, a little loose change?
He does it like it's been done a hundred times
and it's not worth your time or money, but
Oh Sister, is he not a brother to you?

AGM

After Roethke

I have known the inexorable sadness of recorded Minutes,
Remorseless thinning over years of lost intent;
Desolation in the Mission Hall's cheapest room,
Immediate death spasm of call to order resolve;
Unshiftable paint-cemented sash, finger in dust
Graffito on piano and double radiator;
All the misery of doodles and coffee rings,
Feline yawn at the sticking point of Item Six;
The unalterable pathos of No Correspondence,
Ritual of election unopposed, report not available,
Yearly repetition of the volunteer's bad grace.
And I have seen the treacle of inertia extrude its grey
Slick down the faces of the formerly spry, ooze
Through the stubborn armoured love of Mister Chairman
Despairing in silence for Any Item of Other Business.

Acknowledgements are due to the editors of the following publications in which some of these poems first appeared: *Aireings, Critical Survey, Dreamcatcher, The Frogmore Papers, The Interpreter's House, Iota, London Magazine, Orbis, Other Poetry, Poetry Nottingham, Smiths Knoll, Staple, The Swansea Review, Tears In The Fence, Tripod, Ver Poets* and *Ware Poets*.

Thanks to Alan Baker and Clive Allen for Real Art wisdom over the years.